Scriptures That Safeguard Marriage Workbook.

By Rev. James Graham

This picture book was a pleasure to put together. The wonderful institution of marriage is a magnificent centerpiece God has put together for humanity. As I was gathering "Scriptures that Safeguard Marriage", I began to notice four recurring themes scripture highlighted. The First Theme being, *The Definition of Marriage and God's view of it.* The Second Theme being, *The Sacrificial Husband and his duties to his wife.* The Third Theme being, *The Submissive Wife and her duties to her husband.* Lastly, The Fourth Theme being, *Monogamy and Faithfulness between Husband and Wife in the eyes of God.* I pray that this publication helps and enhance Godly Marriages around our country. Be Blessed.

THE 4 THEMES OF BIBLICAL MARRIAGE

	The First Theme: The Definition of Marriage and God's view of it.	
The Second Theme: The Sacrificial Husband and his duties to his wife.		**The Third Theme:** The Submissive Wife and her duties to her husband.
	The Fourth Theme: Monogamy and Faithfulness between Husband and Wife.	

"Where to find the Scriptures I need?"

The First Theme: The Definition of Marriage and God's view of it.
Page 1, Page 3, Page 19, Page 21, Page 23, Page 39, and Page 41

The Second Theme: The Sacrificial Husband and his duties to his wife.
Page 5, Page 9, Page 11, Page 15, Page 17, Page 25, Page 29, Page 31, and Page 33

The Third Theme: The Submissive Wife and her duties to her husband.
Page 7, Page 13, and Page 27

The Fourth Theme: Monogamy and Faithfulness between Husband and Wife.
Page 35 and Page 37

And Adam said, This *is* now bone of my bones, and flesh of my flesh: she shall be called Woman, because she was taken out of Man. -Genesis 2:23

The First Theme: The Definition of Marriage and God's View of it.

Work Time!

"Now is the time to discuss the scripture from the previous page and relate it to your own marriage!"

(Please pick from the 4 categories to begin the conversation.)

- Understand Completely
- Can't Identify
- Don't Understand
- Don't Agree with

What He said.	What She said.

**End each discussion Thanking God for your Marriage
and the maturity that will follow!**

Therefore shall a man leave his father and his mother, and shall cleave unto his wife: and they shall be one flesh. -Genesis 2:24

The First Theme: The Definition of Marriage and God's View of it.

Work Time!

"Now is the time to discuss the scripture from the previous page and relate it to your own marriage!"

(Please pick from the 4 categories to begin the conversation.)

- Understand Completely
- Can't Identify
- Don't Understand
- Don't Agree with

What He said.	What She said.

**End each discussion Thanking God for your Marriage
and the maturity that will follow!**

When a man hath taken a new wife, he shall not go out to war, neither shall he be charged with any business: *but* **he shall be free at home one year, and shall cheer up his wife which he hath taken. -Deuteronomy 24:5**

The Second Theme: The Sacrificial Husband and his duties to his wife

Work Time!

"Now is the time to discuss the scripture from the previous page and relate it to your own marriage!"

(Please pick from the 4 categories to begin the conversation.)

- Understand Completely
- Can't Identify
- Don't Understand
- Don't Agree with

What He said.	What She said.

**End each discussion Thanking God for your Marriage
and the maturity that will follow!**

Thy wife *shall be* as a fruitful vine by the sides of thine house: thy children like olive plants round about thy table. -Psalm 128:3

The Third Theme: The Submissive Wife and her duties to her husband

Work Time!

"Now is the time to discuss the scripture from the previous page and relate it to your own marriage!"

(Please pick from the 4 categories to begin the conversation.)

- Understand Completely
- Can't Identify
- Don't Understand
- Don't Agree with

What He said.	What She said.

**End each discussion Thanking God for your Marriage
and the maturity that will follow!**

Let thy fountain be blessed: and rejoice with the wife of thy youth.
-Proverbs 5:18

The Second Theme: The Sacrificial Husband and his duties to his wife

Work Time!

"Now is the time to discuss the scripture from the previous page and relate it to your own marriage!"

(Please pick from the 4 categories to begin the conversation.)

- Understand Completely
- Can't Identify
- Don't Understand
- Don't Agree with

What He said.	What She said.

**End each discussion Thanking God for your Marriage
and the maturity that will follow!**

Whoso findeth a wife findeth a good *thing*, and obtaineth favour of the LORD.
-Proverbs 18:22

The Second Theme: The Sacrificial Husband and his duties to his wife

Work Time!

"Now is the time to discuss the scripture from the previous page and relate it to your own marriage!"

(Please pick from the 4 categories to begin the conversation.)

- Understand Completely
- Can't Identify
- Don't Understand
- Don't Agree with

What He said.	What She said.

**End each discussion Thanking God for your Marriage
and the maturity that will follow!**

House and riches *are* the inheritance of fathers: and a prudent wife *is* from the LORD. -Proverbs 19:14

The Third Theme: The Submissive Wife and her duties to her husband

Work Time!

"Now is the time to discuss the scripture from the previous page and relate it to your own marriage!"

(Please pick from the 4 categories to begin the conversation.)

- Understand Completely
- Can't Identify
- Don't Understand
- Don't Agree with

What He said.	What She said.

**End each discussion Thanking God for your Marriage
and the maturity that will follow!**

And did not he make one? Yet had he the residue of the spirit. And wherefore one? That he might seek a godly seed. Therefore take heed to your spirit, and let none deal treacherously against the wife of his youth. -Malachi 2:15

The Second Theme: The Sacrificial Husband and his duties to his wife

Work Time!

"Now is the time to discuss the scripture from the previous page and relate it to your own marriage!"

(Please pick from the 4 categories to begin the conversation.)

- Understand Completely
- Can't Identify
- Don't Understand
- Don't Agree with

What He said.	What She said.

**End each discussion Thanking God for your Marriage
and the maturity that will follow!**

Let the husband render unto the wife due benevolence: and likewise also the wife unto the husband. - 1 Corinthians 7:3

The Second Theme: The Sacrificial Husband and his duties to his wife

Work Time!

"Now is the time to discuss the scripture from the previous page and relate it to your own marriage!"

(Please pick from the 4 categories to begin the conversation.)

- Understand Completely
- Can't Identify
- Don't Understand
- Don't Agree with

What He said.	What She said.

**End each discussion Thanking God for your Marriage
and the maturity that will follow!**

The wife hath not power of her own body, but the husband: and likewise also the husband hath not power of his own body, but the wife. -1 Corinthians 7:4

The First Theme: The Definition of Marriage and God's View of it.

Work Time!

"Now is the time to discuss the scripture from the previous page and relate it to your own marriage!"

(Please pick from the 4 categories to begin the conversation.)

- Understand Completely
- Can't Identify
- Don't Understand
- Don't Agree with

What He said.	What She said.

**End each discussion Thanking God for your Marriage
and the maturity that will follow!**

But if they cannot contain, let them marry: for it is better to marry than to burn.
- 1 Corinthians 7:10

The First Theme: The Definition of Marriage and God's View of it.

Work Time!

"Now is the time to discuss the scripture from the previous page and relate it to your own marriage!"

(Please pick from the 4 categories to begin the conversation.)

- Understand Completely
- Can't Identify
- Don't Understand
- Don't Agree with

What He said.	What She said.

End each discussion Thanking God for your Marriage and the maturity that will follow!

Charity suffereth long, *and* is kind; charity envieth not; charity vaunteth not itself, is not puffed up, Doth not behave itself unseemly, seeketh not her own, is not easily provoked, thinketh no evil; Rejoiceth not in iniquity, but rejoiceth in the truth; Beareth all things, believeth all things, hopeth all things, endureth all things. - 1 Corinthians 13:4-7

The First Theme: The Definition of Marriage and God's View of it

Work Time!

"Now is the time to discuss the scripture from the previous page and relate it to your own marriage!"

(Please pick from the 4 categories to begin the conversation.)

- Understand Completely
- Can't Identify
- Don't Understand
- Don't Agree with

What He said.	What She said.

**End each discussion Thanking God for your Marriage
and the maturity that will follow!**

For the husband is the head of the wife, even as Christ is the head of the church: and he is the saviour of the body. -Ephesians 5:23

The Second Theme: The Sacrificial Husband and his duties to his wife

Work Time!

"Now is the time to discuss the scripture from the previous page and relate it to your own marriage!"

(Please pick from the 4 categories to begin the conversation.)

- Understand Completely
- Can't Identify
- Don't Understand
- Don't Agree with

What He said.	What She said.

**End each discussion Thanking God for your Marriage
and the maturity that will follow!**

Therefore as the church is subject unto Christ, so *let* the wives *be* to their own husbands in everything. -Ephesians 5:24

The Third Theme: The Submissive Wife and her duties to her husband

Work Time!

"Now is the time to discuss the scripture from the previous page and relate it to your own marriage!"

(Please pick from the 4 categories to begin the conversation.)

- Understand Completely
- Can't Identify
- Don't Understand
- Don't Agree with

What He said.	What She said.

**End each discussion Thanking God for your Marriage
and the maturity that will follow!**

Husbands, love your wives, even as Christ also loved the church, and gave himself for it; -Ephesians 5:25

The Second Theme: The Sacrificial Husband and his duties to his wife

Work Time!

"Now is the time to discuss the scripture from the previous page and relate it to your own marriage!"

(Please pick from the 4 categories to begin the conversation.)

- Understand Completely
- Can't Identify
- Don't Understand
- Don't Agree with

What He said.	What She said.

End each discussion Thanking God for your Marriage and the maturity that will follow!

So ought men to love their wives as their own bodies. He that loveth his wife loveth himself -Ephesians 5:28

The Second Theme: The Sacrificial Husband and his duties to his wife

Work Time!

"Now is the time to discuss the scripture from the previous page and relate it to your own marriage!"

(Please pick from the 4 categories to begin the conversation.)

- Understand Completely
- Can't Identify
- Don't Understand
- Don't Agree with

What He said.	What She said.

End each discussion Thanking God for your Marriage and the maturity that will follow!

Nevertheless let every one of you in particular so love his wife even as himself; and the wife *see* that she reverence *her* husband. Ephesians 5:33

The Second Theme: The Sacrificial Husband and his duties to his wife

Work Time!

"Now is the time to discuss the scripture from the previous page and relate it to your own marriage!"

(Please pick from the 4 categories to begin the conversation.)

- Understand Completely
- Can't Identify
- Don't Understand
- Don't Agree with

What He said.	What She said.

**End each discussion Thanking God for your Marriage
and the maturity that will follow!**

A bishop then must be blameless, the husband of <u>one wife</u>, vigilant, sober, of good behaviour, given to hospitality, apt to teach; - 1 Timothy 3:2

The Fourth Theme: Monogamy and Faithfulness between Husband and Wife

Work Time!

"Now is the time to discuss the scripture from the previous page and relate it to your own marriage!"

(Please pick from the 4 categories to begin the conversation.)

- Understand Completely
- Can't Identify
- Don't Understand
- Don't Agree with

What He said.	What She said.

**End each discussion Thanking God for your Marriage
and the maturity that will follow!**

If any be blameless, the husband of <u>one wife</u>, having faithful children not accused of riot or unruly. - Titus 1:6

The Fourth Theme: Monogamy and Faithfulness between Husband and Wife

Work Time!

"Now is the time to discuss the scripture from the previous page and relate it to your own marriage!"

(Please pick from the 4 categories to begin the conversation.)

- Understand Completely
- Can't Identify
- Don't Understand
- Don't Agree with

What He said.	What She said.

End each discussion Thanking God for your Marriage and the maturity that will follow!

Marriage is honourable in all, and the bed undefiled: but whoremongers and adulterers God will judge. -Hebrews 13:4

The First Theme: The Definition of Marriage and God's View of it.

Work Time!

"Now is the time to discuss the scripture from the previous page and relate it to your own marriage!"

(Please pick from the 4 categories to begin the conversation.)

- Understand Completely
- Can't Identify
- Don't Understand
- Don't Agree with

What He said.	What She said.

**End each discussion Thanking God for your Marriage
and the maturity that will follow!**

Likewise, ye husbands, dwell with them according to knowledge, giving honour unto the wife, as unto the weaker vessel, and as being heirs together of the grace of life; that your prayers be not hindered. -1 Peter 3:7

The First Theme: The Definition of Marriage and God's View of it

THE TOP 12 MONOGAMOUS MARRIAGES OF THE BIBLE

THE TOP 12 MONOGAMOUS MARRIAGES OF THE BIBLE

1. Adam and Eve: *Genesis 2:23, 3:20, and 4:1*
2. Isaac and Rebekah: *Genesis 24:20 and 24:64-67*
3. Joseph and Asenath: *Genesis 41:45 and 41:50*
4. Amram and Jechebed: *Exodus 6:20*
5. Aaron and Elisheba: *Exodus 6:23*
6. Moses and Zipporah: *Exodus 2:21 and 4:25-26*
7. Lippidoth and Deborah: *Judges 4:4*
8. Boaz and Ruth: *Ruth 4:13*
9. Shallum and Huldah: *2 Chronicles 34:22*
10. Zechariah and Elizabeth: *Luke 1:5-6*
11. Joseph and Mary: *Matthew 1:20*
12. Aquila and Priscilla: *Acts 18:2*

www.ingramcontent.com/pod-product-compliance
Lightning Source LLC
Chambersburg PA
CBHW080046260726
48658CB00007B/2769